EPIPHANY-LOVE.COM
WISDOM for INTRINSIC FULFILLMENT
AUTHOR: WILLA R. BOYKIN

STUDY, LEARN, TEACH, MASTERY and EXCELLENCE

DIFFERENT RESULTS REQUIRES A Paradigm Shift

A CALL TO ACTION

ENTREPRENEUR OWNERSHIP IS BETTER

LOVE CONQUERS ALL

SKILLS ATTRIBUTES & CHARACTER

COMMUNICATION WORKS

DIVERSITY

A WINNING ATTITUDE

BALANCED LIFESTYLE

REWARDED

Wisdom Publication
wb@epiphany.com
Copyrights 2009

Epiphany-Love LLC
P. O. Box 53580
Cincinnati, Ohio 45253

Copyright © 2009 Willa R. Boykin
All rights reserved.

ISBN: 0-9765329-0-5
ISBN-13: 9780976532903

Visit www.createspace.com/1000247870 to order additional copies.

Table of Contents

Website (Cover)

Wisdom	1
Better Known as Student Loan's	2
Begin to Transform Problem Solving	4
Diverse People	5
Epiphany definition	6
Intrinsic definition	7
Introduction: Wisdom for Intrinsic Fulfillment	9
Foreword: (Pearl Jordan)	11
We Must Remember They Need to Know	13
U. S. Capitol Building Washington, D. C.	14
U. S. White House Washington D. C.	15
Life Skills On Your Mark, Get Set, Head Start K-8	17
On Your Mark, Get Set, Head Start K-8	18
Life Skills Youth Educational Venture 9–12 Grades	20
Youth Educational Venture 9–12 Grades	21
Life skills Morals, Values, and Goals	22
Morals, Values and Goals (Both Feet Inbound)	23
Life Skills Goals, Dreams and Evaluation	24
Goals, Dreams and Evaluation	25
Life Skills Communication	27
Communication	28
Like Skills Education The Tassel is Worth the Hassle	30
Education–The Tassel is Worth the Hassle	31
Life Skills Creativity and Talents–Finding your Greatest Assets (Your Calling)	32

Creativity and Talents–Finding your Greatest Asset (Your Calling)	33
Life Skills Formula for Achieving Goals	35
Formula for Achieving Goals	36
Life Skills Divine Awareness and Expectancy	37
Success–Divine Awareness and Divine Expectancy	38
Life Skills A Salute United States Military and Veterans	39
A Salute to our United States Military and Veterans	40
Life Skills Perseverance–Workplace and Volunteerism	42
Perseverance Workplace and Volunteerism	43
Life Skills The Perfect Role Model	45
The Perfect Role Model	46
Life Skills Winners	48
Winners	49
Life Skills Entrepreneur	50
Entrepreneur–A Glimpse into Ownership and Wealth	51
CEO and Entrepreneur Summit	52
Own Your Future	53
Life Skills Diversity	54
Diversity	55
Life Skills Seniors are Precious Assets	56
Seniors are Precious Assets	57
Life skills African and American History/Who are you?	58
African and American History/Who are you?	59
Life Skills Death–The Loss of Someone Special	61
Death–The Loss of Someone Special	62
Life Skills Parenting	64
Parenting	65
Life skills Children and Adults Challenged Survivor Techniques	67

Children and Adults Physical Challenged Survivor Techniques	68
Life Skills Anger Management–A Wise Man Controls Anger	70
Anger Management–A Wise Man Controls Anger	71
Life Skills a Sound Mind	73
A Sound Mind	74
Life Skills Wellness/Emotional and Physical	76
Wellness–Emotional and Physical	77
Life Skills A Moment in Time	79
A Moment in Time	80
If I Can Teach Important Life Skills	81
Survey Questionnaire	82

WISDOM

A collections of thoughts and ideas base on your ability to discern what is true or right to make sound judgement after discernment.

Insight or Intuition. Common Sense.

A high degree of knowledge or learning.

An accumulated body of knowledge, as in philosophy or science, etc.

☙

COLLEGE STUDENT STRESS
BETTER KNOWN AS STUDENT LOAN'S
CAN INTERFERE AND POSTPONE PROGRESS

Most of your colleague or associates familiarize stress as, it's common place to the words Student Loan's. For most of you it will not take a back seat and it's a hostage holder on your college profile. It also holds you to a time line after finishing college and those interest rates may cause you sleepless nights. Consider for one moment what could happen to your credit score? Imagine your college profile being over shadowed in student loan's. Your many accomplishments are merits, and not to be robbed center stage.

Five important tips that I would like to leave with you for student loan's are commonly repeated practices and procedures. First, there is the worry factor, an all too common gambling struggle. Second, your child can work toward college credits while still in high school. Third, if possible, maybe volunteer for legal community projects, government projects (Seahawk) and business opportunities to earn a reduced college course credit. Fourth, check for scholarships, pell grants and tuition assistance programs. Last, parents can open a 529 Savings Account for their children's college. The awareness factor and being proactive oppose to reactive will definitely help towards parent and child relationship.

There are ways to avoid the rising cost associated with student loan's. You may seek to volunteer a portion of your time to serve on orientation recorded jobs. You may also consider the federal government or Armed Forces. Corporate America has a plan to help qualify your needs or desires that include less paper work and target passing grades while employed. Corporate will offer you life time training benefits for as long as you are their employee. If you become part of a restructuring downsizing group you may qualify for education benefits to began a new career path. Don't forget book keeping while attending college to cut back on nails, hair salons, tattoo's, cell phone usage and fashions.

Of course some of us can always count on our parents to pick up the tabs. I think it's wonderful when parents set aside college tuition for their children to further advance their knowledge. It happens all the time. We need parents more than ever before to plan in advance for their student's college education after high school. The mind is a terrible asset to waste. Education is a life long process and we learn something new or we need to modify our daily interactions with one another.

I sometimes think what if your student loan's were reduced because you bought a college sports seasonal pass? Suppose your employer and union were to establish a plan, after completing five years, to reduce some student loan's accumulated before you entered their workforce? I can help you to brain storm your way to several possible solutions. America has your back!

Wisdom for Intrinsic Fulfillment

Begin to transform problem solving using wisdom, patience, and applying the application of knowledge

Has your circumstances; environment, attitude or crises caused you instability?

Discover physical and spiritual power within yourself to make simple modifications.

Explore the basic foundation of wellness, work and play as you interact with others.

Wisdom for Intrinsic Fulfillment is a reference guide irrespective of age and race. It's intended to assist transition individuals and families to achieve a wholesome lifestyle.

༄

Not only are people who genuinely

feel committed to a cause for the

good of humanity diverse, but also

they're the luckiest people in the world

EPIPHANY–Company Name

e-piph-a-ny

"I experienced an epiphany, a spiritual flash that would change the way I viewed myself"

A sudden manifestation of the essence or meaning of something. A comprehension or perception of a sudden intuitive realization.

in-trin-sic

He was better qualified than they to estimate justly the intrinsic value of Grecian philosophy and refinement. -I. Taylor

Inward; internal; hence; true; genuine; real; essential; inherent; not merely apparent or accidental; -opposed to extrinsic;' as the intrinsic worth of goodness of a person.

Belonging to a thing by its very nature; "form was treated as something intrinsic, as the very essence of the thing" –John Dewey

Situated within or belonging solely to the organ or body part on which it acts

༄

INTRODUCTION

Welcome to Wisdom for Intrinsic Fulfillment. My name is Willa, and I am a native of Cincinnati, Ohio. I am a former telecommunication's employee with thirty-five years served. When I consider a positive world class goal and a positive world class approach, emphasis are placed on positive behavior and solutions with a bright future.

The workbook study course is aimed at study, learn, teach and mastery. Bad habits will show up when you least expect them. Good habits will lead to mastery, and mastery will always lead to excellence. Wisdom for Intrinsic Fulfillment is fun, super simple and has a variety of twenty-four topics for discussions. It is also designed to teach awareness of important life skills to correspond with each topic. Developing skilled attributes that mirror our character takes center stage. Relationship's are needed, a smile is an integral part of relationships. Deciding to pursue negative behavior, and not addressing or correcting key elements may not prove favorable.

Epiphany-Love wants to improve lifestyle habits based on test and proven results. Epiphany does not invent but spotlights positive behavior moving forward.

Positive dreamers share a common bond. They share their heart in so many special ways. Its as though the spotlight never left and its brighter than ever. Their dream is bigger than anyone could have ever imagined. Don't make the mistake of thinking I can accomplish my goals alone. Talents and creative gifts are given at birth. They are free to all and powerful. My goal is to walk in the fruits of the Spirit.

EPIPHANY-LOVE will also donate a portion of its profits to charity. Cincinnati Children's Hospital and Northern Kentucky University, Chase Law School. No other assessments are factored into your cost, and there is no buying remorse.

We can become team winner's when we engage in making a difference, assisting others to maturity and rewarding improvements. There's nothing more creative than the discovery of a purposeful lifestyle.

Getting started with writing on the computer did not come easy. I thought this is not working out, but I kept up the pace. What was

Introduction: Wisdom for Intrinsic Fulfillment

I going to do with all this paper besides throwing it away? Well, one day I had an EPIPHANY (company name) or light bulb moment and things begin to brighten. My dream became half circle. Why not write about my life experiences to share and help others in similar circumstances. Education is a life long process where we rise and fall to new ideas daily. After much consideration and proven results, I can report that wisdom, patience and applying the application of knowledge led me to my next level. (A Call to Action)

Thank you and I hope you will find the study course beneficial for you, your family, extended family and friends.

FOREWORD

Willa has been a Super Hero for me twenty-five plus years. I first met her and her family when she and her husband bought their first home next door to our family. She possesses high moral standards. There was never any question about what she was striving to do. Willa lives the kind of life that is clearly seen as an example for others to follow. She practices what she talks about or what she preaches. She is a student and doer of the Word. Her children, family, church family, extended family and friends have embraced her teachings.

It is no wonder that she has written a book that outline step by step the procedures for living a good and "wholesome" life, that is to put it in Willa's own words. She is not only an example for her family and friends but the communities of the world to follow.

How many people do you know personally that have sat down and thought about what you would like to see in people's actions and re-actions on a given day or in a granted situation? This booklet could be used as a prerequisite or intertwined with the curriculum of schools, Sunday schools, summer day camps, or other situations where one could reach a broad audience to instruct and in form young minds and old alike.

Our society is in a state of disrepair at this time. For whatever reason the standards up held by our parents, have taken a backseat to patterns of behavior that promote devastation of our Creator's will. Where do we go from here to repair the damage that has been and keep us moving in an onward direction? Let us set this time, the year 2008 twenty-first century, as our beginning movement of change. Look positively at the number of persons we can impact. Willa's outline can and will change the direction of our nation one person at a time.

It is material and works like this that will take us back to a society that respect the reason for being and a great nation. Love unconditionally is free, rewarding, the will for all men and never returns void. When we learn to obey and keep these teachings we will see change in Our-selves, our Communities, our State our United States and the World.

Foreword: (Pearl Jordan)

I say Willa Boykin's work is a timely piece of work that will help move us in a forward direction for the good of everyone. POWERFUL STUFF

Pearl Rogers Jordan
Retired Public School License Educator

We must remember they need to know

When you win we all win

Replace anger with an education

To fear the unknown of diversity is real

Diverse people are more open minded

Education is a one way ticket to your next level

If you ask for a good day chances are you receive it

United we stand together but divided we fall together

Two kinds of people
Those people who know that they don't know
Those people who think they know but they don't know

Giving is receiving, smile and have a nice day

Different results requires a different approach

We rise and fall to new ideas daily

A moment in time recognize and seize the opportunity

U. S. Capitol Building Washington, D. C.

(Capitol)

U. S. White House Washington D. C.

(White House)

IMPORTANT LIFE SKILLS

On Your Mark, Get Set, Head Start K-8

Believe in yourself

You do things because it's the right thing to do

Create and restore relationships

Earn both an education and rewarded to your next level

A win-win process for both the child and the faculty

Develop good listening skills and learn to think and rethink before answering. Maybe it will improve your chance to answer correctly.

Welcome to a world filled with diversity

The only stupid questions are the ones that were never asked

Become a team player

As the world turns, the people in the world will view the opportunities and it's future existence.

༄

America Has Your Back!

On Your Mark, Get Set, Head Start K-8

I like myself, I believe that I'm created to be special, talented, smart, beautiful, loving and I bear no shame

As an American citizen I walk with dignity, humbleness and I know the meaning of my name

Would you like to hear me sing the alphabetic song?
I use to sing songs with my parents, but now I can do it on my own

First grade is the time of year when we must practice getting into full gear
Reading, writing, mathematic and friendship will be the main curriculum of this year

More challenges as a second grader, computers, internet and no more digital divides
Rules are very important as I navigate in search of answers to what it provides

Under supervision I will be introduced to my school and neighborhood libraries
Blue prints, fiction, non fiction, dictionaries, the Mighty Mississippi and all of its tributaries

Anticipation seems to describe third grade as we explore the map of our city
City Hall, Museum Center, Freedom Center and zoo becomes off campus studies

It's a pleasure for me to share with you information on the state in which I live
The state seal, its capitol location, agriculture, industries, natural resources and population, I'm prepared to give

Fifth graders understand the positive effects of becoming a team player and dedication
The United States, a free nation; democracy and American History teaches me to appreciate an education

Its important that I know and understand global markets if I choose to make my pitch
Understanding imports, exports, tariffs, and currency may help me to find my niche

My teachers have articulated, illustrated and tested me on the lessons to make sure that I have learned
Educators seem to have a passion for helping all students and a genuine concern

We are all unique, that includes diversity, beautiful skin colors and DNA's to distinguish one from another
An incredible planned design for empowerment and to assist me as well as others

༄

America Has Your Back!

IMPORTANT LIFE SKILLS

Youth Education Venture 9–12 Grades

Believe in yourself

You do things because it's the right thing to do and it can make a difference

As the world turns and the people in the world view changes differently opportunities will exist

Develop good listening skills and learn to think and re-think

Develop a winning attitude. Repeat gratification will support you with high marks.

Learn to read the lines, read in between the lines and learn to read beyond the lines.

༄

America Has Your Back!

Youth Educational Venture 9–12 Grades

You are the next generation of leaders. You are our future hope for tomorrow. You will carry the torch that represents freedom, unity, love and peace for America and the universe. You will lead this nation based on its principles, with dignity and respect. You must seek ways to prepare yourself for tomorrow's occupations. The world will come to know you as a strong society, compassionate and determined to resolve issues in our homeland and abroad.

Grade 9	Grade 10	Grade 11	Grade 12
Freedom	America	Tomorrow's Occupations	Strong Society
Unity	Dignity		
Love	Humble	Hope	America
Peace	Writing	America	Determine
America	Speaking	Life Skills	World
Life Skills	Life Skills	Writing	Mastery
			Writing
			Speaking

America Has Your Back!

IMPORTANT LIFE SKILLS

Morals, Values and Goals

You do things because it's the right thing to do, alway listen to your inter voice

Ask yourself why as often as needed and the how will come later

If you want to get ahead in life you must set goals

Morals and Values are precious gem stones, always guard, protect and claim ownership

Create and restore relationships

To function properly you need to practice giving, receiving and a smile

༄

When you find yourself off course remember that both feet inbound always helps to guide our path

Morals, Values and Goals (Both Feet Inbound)

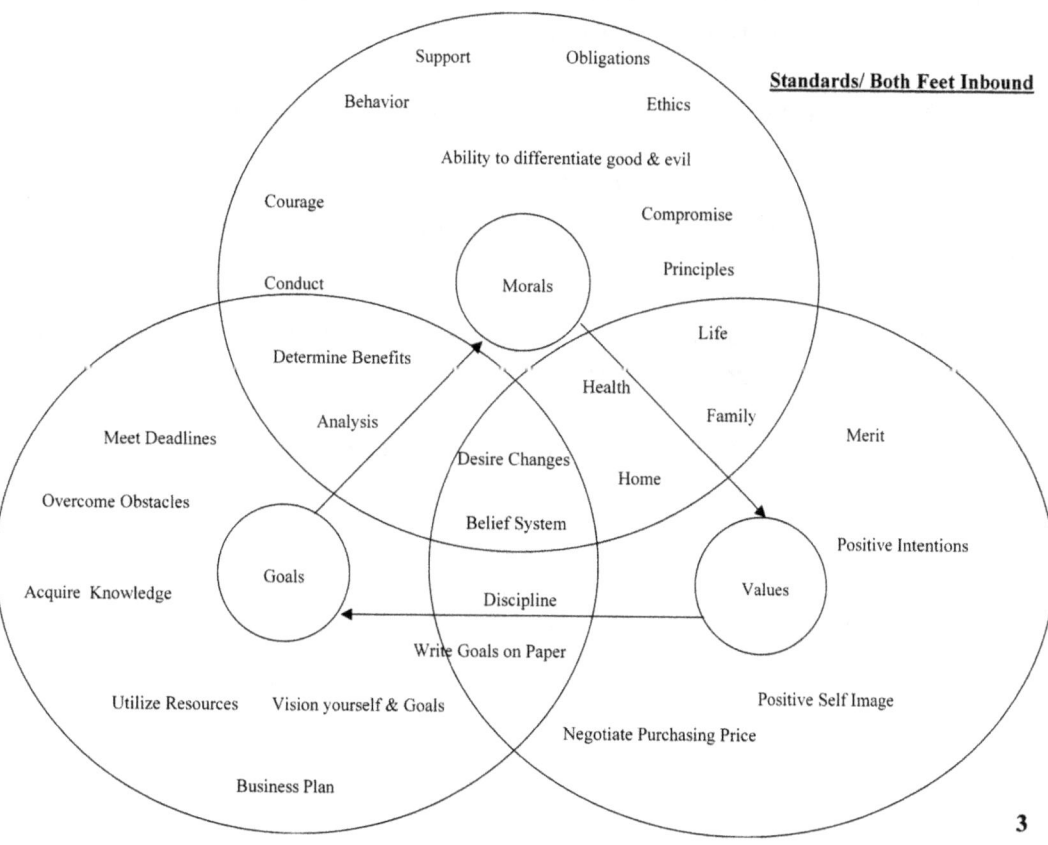

Standards/ Both Feet Inbound

3

IMPORTANT LIFE SKILLS

Goals, Dreams and Evaluation

You do things because it's the right thing to do. Never because it is what it is.

Training, development and education must occur.

An action plan that includes communication and presentation skills lends to the solution.

You win and we all win. What is it that I need to do?

It's not wise to share your dream with everyone. Be encouraged to interpret your dream and family members show respect.

Dreamers vision ways to bridge the gap between one another's unfinished dream

Always ask yourself and double check to make sure you are on the correct path

Goals, Dreams and Evaluation

An individual known as a dreamer may experience dreaming several times during the week. Dreamer's who are gifted with interpretation are regarded as special. Its not uncommon for the dream to become true or perhaps a warning of some sort. No one can predict how long it will take before manifestation. Generally dreamers are sought after and may be offered a large sum for their services. They are not to be mistaken for a fortune teller.

Dreamers feel better after all the pieces to the puzzle have been placed correctly. They're familiar with walking in love and being true to the mission. A dreamer has taken the time to map out his course and determined that there are no quick fixes. Heavy opposition may arise due to no clear understanding of the mission or can't agree. The mastermind, in a calm voice will begin to speak and we sense he's familiar with his dream. Mindful of weathering storms, their ability to recognize a problem and assist in solving the problem suggest an accomplish.

It's very important that we show and give them respect and don't become jealous. It may very well be associated within the spiritual realm and heaven. You may want to follow your dream and purpose to see where it leads you. Interpretation may be years away and not apparent until time is ready to reveal. A natural truth, a wonderland, honesty and love deserves merit. Maybe its intended for you only. A dream can represent a miracle and take you places you've never been before.

I've never experience a life of achievements without setting goals for my self. They help you to organize and see your direction path. Personal documentation is readily available for measuring and progress. I find it true and a lot easier if you believe you can and picture yourself as an achiever. It's wise and a good habit to replace accomplished goals with new goals. It helps you to maintain balance. Goals are important and plays a major role in improving your potential, extending arms, and assisting you to a new level.

There are two types of goals. A give-up goal, and a go-up goal. Familiarize and test yourself so that you will understand and distinguish their

Goals, Dreams and Evaluation

differences. It allows you to view why not share and when to share. Don't be ashamed if you have big or multi goals, it will only get better.

It's time to evaluate or take inventory of yourself. Life is not always easy and not always fair. Being hard on yourself makes life a bit easier for you. Education is a life long process where we learn to implement those important decision and strive to advance to the next level.

∽

IMPORTANT LIFE SKILLS

Communication

Speak what is true, honest, just, pure, lovely and of a good report, and you will never be lost for words

Communication works

Character manifest effectiveness

A good listener plays a major role in good communication

A good communicator is not afraid of a dialogue

Your opinion is not the only one that matters to the team

Disagree professional when you feel strongly that solution A oppose to solution C is the best solution

Clear communication and presentation skills lend to the solution

Communication

Communication begins with the spoken word and song. Our intelligence will received a boost from learning to use our five senses. The spoken word penetrates depth, breadth, convictions and wisdom. The written word will always come later.

Communication generates ideas and data. Data can be transferred into information. In turn information goes through a processing cycle of verification, analyses and evaluation. It can be presented as formal or informal information. Afterwards, information can safely be transformed into applied knowledge, and ready for usage. Accountability and trust after being informed may include recommendations.

Communication is effective when the sender encodes a thought and the receiver is able to decode the thought correctly. The receiver may not understand the message, therefore communication from the sender may be transmitted differently. A breakthrough offers the sender a significant opportunity to change course. The sender must create the correct atmosphere for the subject matter.

The twenty-first century or the recommendation age offers a broader range of communications technology. Home phone usage will decline as broadband and wireless communication will become dominant. The internet usage will increase and newspapers will show a decline. The information age has been replaced. Voice over IP (internet protocol) means you now have access simultaneous to your phone and the internet. Text messaging, e-mail, movies, games, pictures and cameras are normal activities over the phone. By in large, the oldest effective means of communication, AT&T remains some carriers had to change names. The United States Post Office now threaten by the internet still remains.

Effective communication does not exist when the blame game and false pretense are present. You may have heard the one who speaks the loudest is the one who gets heard. It does not indicate that they are right, but someone decided not to voice an opinion. Communication transmit news, ideas and feelings. It must be processed promptly. "Yesterday's news is history."

More often you want to create a dialogue instead of a monologue. Proper communication will sometimes end in disagreement. Our posture, gestures, enthusiasm, eye contact, appearance and tone of voice will send a message to the receiver. First impressions seem to last. A communicator may not always agree with the subject matter, but he is skilled at relaying the information and facilitating discussions. The communicator must develop creditability, sincerity, the art of persuasion and establish a good rapport.

IMPORTANT LIFE SKILLS

Education–The Tassel is Worth the Hassle

Believe in yourself and turning back is not an option

There are many different and nontraditional ways to achieve an education

Education is a life long process where we rise and fall to new and old ideas daily

Your ability to achieve and to reach your potential or surpass all expectations is not uncommon

Empower and surround yourself with positive people working on improving their lifestyle

America Has Your Back!

EDUCATION

The Tassel is Worth the Hassle

Education can start as early as eight weeks old on potty training. My beloved mother devoted to serve her grandchildren performed this training. I reviewed eye witness accounts that it's possible and achievable. You begin training immediately after the infant awakens. They always go during this period and you teach them sound. A one and a half year old child can begin his education through the spoken word. The spoken words came first, but the written words will always come years later.

Formal education starts with the use of our five senses, sound, smell, sight, movements, objects and song. We will never stop learning, that's because our mind, spirit and body are dependents. Education is introduce as formal, instructional, schooling, support groups, training, nontraditional, self experienced and mass media. Education is the foundation that governs.

Those having received some form of training or education will develop a tendency to become well-rounded and adaptable to change. An education will be viewed by many as a valuable investment. It travels with you everywhere you go, it cannot be stolen, provides comment and analogies attributed to life.

Information is stored in our brain's memory bank. After learning has taken place, you may retrieve or speed up the process to review stored information. To assure education equality the big picture must be identifiable and studied by legislators. Afterwards legislation must outline improvements and necessary steps can be implemented into law.

Playing on a level field may requirer more persistence. You believe and you know that location "B" exist, and it may take you longer or a detour to arrive there. Consider arrival and consensus that I have earned respect to be there and the same opportunities to accomplish my dreams does exist. It becomes inevitable that I choose to study, to learn and to master. Learning becomes difficult if you have experience bias or prejudice. Don't be persuaded to give up, you can achieve your dream. Congratulations!

America Has Your Back!

IMPORTANT LIFE SKILLS

Creativity and Talents–Finding your Greatest Asset (Your Calling)

It may be hard to comprehend but your gifts and talents were establish before your birth. We are known before we are born. Nothing just happens and it's not just luck or co-incidental.

Dream on and I'll see you at the top because of your patience things were reveal.

Your gifts and talents are duplicated and shared with other human beings. Beauty was not given to just one person, but it is well distributed. You must be thankful for your assets and learn to use your calling.

To be highly favored is a gift.

Gifts and talents are better used oppose to just placed on the shelf as a dust collector.

If you know of a dreamer or maybe a family member is a dreamer don't plot to destroy him. It's a gift and a blessing.

If we really decided to count our blessings one by one we need to allocate and plan our time.

Creativity and Talents–Finding your Greatest Asset (Your Calling)

Everyone has received a unique gift to use on earth. Some of us are multitalented. We also received power to achieve wealth though creativity and talents. Often times, uniqueness can be easily identified because of its outward appearance. Other gifts are inward and may take more time to uncover.

Often times someone will becomes jealous or resentful of another individual's gift. Being inspired by another's accomplishments will help you to achieve your goals. Sometimes unaware, we reject our gifts because it's not what we had in mind. Before promoting you to the next level, you may have to be trained for preparation, perfection and strengthening through trials. Listening to your inter conscious may help to reveal your purpose in life. It was never intended for our gift to set idle on the shelf because we can't figure out where to place the pieces in the puzzle.

You typically have to go through a molding process. Remove all limitations from yourself, and don't become boxed into an image cover up. Stay focused, sharing your most secret desires from your heart or your dream with the public is not always wise. Persistence, determination, belief and hard work will help you to reach your goals. Often times the same gift will be duplicated and received by others, its not a wise decision to boast and brag.

Personal desires should not be your only focal point, but consider that which is gratifying. You must be willing to cross boundary lines to reach new horizons. Its always wise to consider a new way of using your gift. It's normal to dream and have visions. A dream may be worth implementation.

Never under estimate or think your talents are worthless or non-profitable. Your gift may be parenting, the glue that holds the family together, or a genuine personality, or being an adorable spouse, and the ability to think and lead. Your gift may be in your hands, eyes, feet, ears, voice, appearance, reading, writing, hair, beauty and most important of all is your heart. Your gift may be to establish a new relationship with others.

Creativity and Talents–Finding your Greatest Asset (Your Calling)

Remember you did not give yourself the gift or talent, but you received it to use so that others might see, for you to receive wealth, for others to embrace their own visions and admire the possibilities.

You never know who's watching so be on good behavior. There are others who would like to possess what you already have. Remember you must learn how to be a good steward over your present gifts before receiving additional ones. Always honor and give recognition to those who assisted and helped you to achieve. Enjoy and have fun if possible. Using your gift to intervene on behalf of another may unlock the door to harmony and recovery.

IMPORTANT LIFE SKILLS

Formula for Achieving Goals

Believe in yourself

An organized and direction chart must occur

A balanced lifestyle is important. We are never 100% balanced always

Hurdles & Opportunities make up 50% of the equation

Organization and Directions accounts for 25% each

Entrepreneur's ownership is better

Character manifest effectiveness

Wisdom for Intrinsic Fulfillment–plan, study, learn, teach, mastery and excellence.

Practice positive habits it enables you to achieve excellence

Skilled Attributes are necessary and will show up in our character

Formula for Achieving Goals

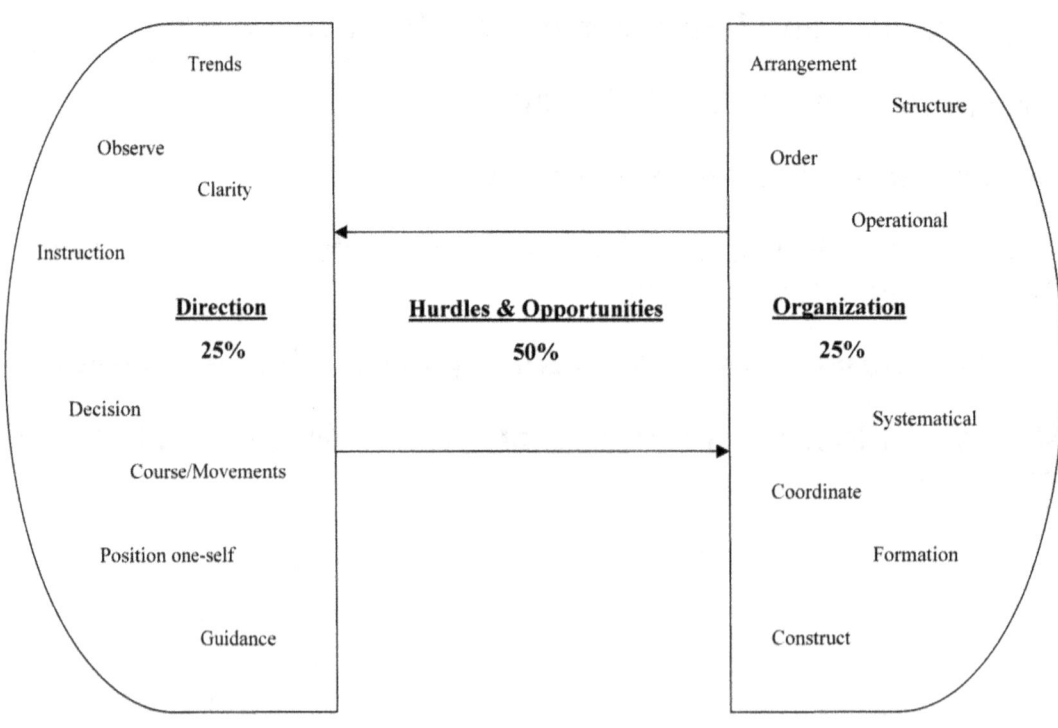

IMPORTANT LIFE SKILLS

Success—Divine Expectancy

Ask for a good day and you will receive it most of the time, life is centered on expectancy

Success is learning to love and forgive one another. Its essential that the foundation is established if your plans include accomplish improvements.

Successful people realize that learning can be traditional, experienced, viewed and nontraditional. Meaning all are effective and acceptable.

Giving is receiving and together they become a powerful endless cycle. Priceless

Familiarize yourself on how to walk humble and tune-up your heart when needed.

Smile, give, receive, ask, knock and seek are essential.

Success or Divine Expectancy

<u>Divine Success Recognizes</u>

"The Law of Harvest" it's a good description of your future

It's not something you accomplish alone

Leaves an inheritance for children and grandchildren

Recognize and replace anger with positive behavior allowing the anger to wear off

Freedom to choose an education oppose to poverty

Love never fails

Builds a positive family relationship, recognizing the whole being greater than its parts

Overcomes evil with good

Develops positive principles to pass on to the next generation

Always knock, ask, and seek, choose the good life and choose eternity

Expect to have a good day and most of the time you will receive a good day

The need to restore order where there is chaos

Fear not obstacles but transforms them into opportunities

We do not always receive what we want, but our needs are never abandon and always met on time

Take pride in planet Earth and help to restore its beauty, wonderlands and habitants

IMPORTANT LIFE SKILLS

A Salute to our United States Military and Veterans

Welcome to a world of diversity, greed and compassion

War is hell. Imagine being position on the frontline of a battlefield, the team should always assist one another.

Well earned respect

Rewards include education benefits

Honored to restore peace for your country and the world

Create and restore relationships

Ceremonial with honors to have served and honorable recognition

∽

We Salute You!

A Salute to our United States Military and Veteran

Because of the various wars that America fought and for those who gave or loss their lives, freedom remains. To the native Americans who introduced their crops and land, may they be remembered for thankful giving. For those who wanted a different form of government, may there be liberty and justice for all. To the slaves crying out freedom over security, let there be accountability and responsibility to all.

One nation and democracy they positioned themselves across the battlefields. On our homeland we share grief in our hearts knowing there is no guarantee that every parent's child sent to war will return home safely. Causalities ran high as they fought hard and sometimes years for America's homeland and world peace keepers.

They are represented by many ethnic backgrounds and they wore various uniforms. Some were drafted and some volunteered. Others desired to travel to see the world, and to someday buy their own homes. In faith they trusted and hope for the good life, to be trained and educated for careers after serving their country. Their reasons are numerous, however they shared a common interest, that America stands ready to protect, preserve and embrace freedom. They also exercised their common nationality of freedom to pray. For some returning home after war meant challenging the United States Constitution, and that it must represent all citizens.

Our United States Constitution represents protection, equality and world class goals. We are a great nation experienced at trying a world class approach. Our mission is to resolve critical issues and that we experience no physical harm by submitting world class resolutions. War is hell filled with torment, revenge, hatred and shame.

America! America! From the Canadian borders and the five great lakes, to the Atlantic Ocean and to the Gulf of Mexico, to the Pacific Ocean and from sea to shinning sea, America's military stands ready. The eagle has landed with his powerful wings and keen eyesight. He has eliminated his predators and brings a message of hope, forgiveness, healing, restoration and prosperity. Liberty and justice for all echoes out as a great protocol. America must continue its stride to be a country of opportunity.

Diversity is alive and well accredited for our remarkable success. Let us remember that the United States Military is a rainbow of colors. Our nation is likewise. As we share in these basic principles, upon which this nation was founded, I salute you for standing tall and united. Let freedom ring throughout this nation and let there be equality for all its citizens.

We must remember those who made the ultimate sacrifice with honors. For those returning home with disabilities they must be cared for with dignity and rehabilitation. With extended arms we welcome you back to America's spirit and the American dream. The foundation has been laid and the price has been paid that we should not abandon our principles of freedom. Truly America is blessed.

We Salute You!

IMPORTANT LIFE SKILLS

Perseverance–Workplace and Volunteerism

Nothing just happens. No one can prevent you from receiving or destroying your creative gifts and talents

You may be blessed with multiple assignments

Show respect and always forgive others

The team is a lot better and effective as a whole

Your efforts will not go unnoticed and does make a difference

Remember those who are less fortunate

Most problems do not vanish, but someone has to take ownership for fixing and resolving the issues.

༺

Perseverance–Workplace and Volunteerism

We have discovered that there are many ways to achieve success. There's only one perfect way; stay committed, be hopeful and be productive. You have successfully learned mastery. No one is an island and wants to stand alone. When you smile the whole world smiles with you but when you frown you are on your own.

Be prompt. Consider arriving ten minutes early. Early arrival is a good habit to practice. The United States has more than one time zone. It also demonstrates courtesy.

Understanding how to budget is important. Always negotiate before making a purchase, it's your money. Learn how to calculate your savings by eliminating interest and credit cards. The lender will always have power over the borrower.

Someone has to recognize and take ownership of a problem. Consider others ideas when you are interacting with them. No one has all the answers and no one wants to be totally left out on problem solving. Start with an analysis of the problem, next is a proposal to identify, present and to study the recommendations as a team. There are key elements in every process that must be identified and studßied and considered before moving forward. Group size is very important in the workplace. Positive enhancements must be included into the equation so feel free to borrow expertise.

While performing your duties in the workplace you may see a shortcut. As long as your performance is done correctly and it does not interfere with another individual's task, developing shortcuts may enhance your productivity. Remember to always be mindful of others. Pay attention to your health, take short breaks and do not skip lunch. This may eliminate feeling overwhelm and overworked.

Volunteerism is a great way to strengthen interactions and development as you begin to venture out of your comfort zone. It allows you to organize your steps and teaches purpose. Teamwork, honesty, trustworthiness, integrity and innovation are exposed. Your purpose is to learn how to follow and to lead. Successful neighborhoods, communities and cities must incorporate the elements of change. As you give of yourself,

Perseverance–Workplace and Volunteerism

time and talents, and share with others you will become the recipient of the greatest reward. The reward being a hidden mystery that tied you and others together are unconditional elements flowing through the process.

Giving is not always represented as money. You may share a hug, sing a song, prepare a meal, possess a positive attitude, or lend a helping hand, give someone a seat, say thank you, give a unit of blood, or a pair of old eyeglasses. It's a good habit to practice when you bless someone else. Giving, receiving and smiling are part of an endless cycle, you will never run out. Have a little fun if circumstances will allow? Stay focus and always remember to perform in a professional manner.

IMPORTANT LIFE SKILLS

The Perfect Role Model

Parents should be observed and recognized as a role model in the home

First impressions seem to last

Learn how to trust your leader to have your best interest in mind

A good leader does not falsify trust, honesty and hope

Believe in yourself. What's right for you may not be viewed with consensus by outsiders

Learn and remember what the leader said to you. Show respect and say, Thank You

Always be fair to the organization you work for and to yourself

The Perfect Role Model

Generally there are two main reasons why an individual should seek to connect and identify with a role model. First we concentrate on their method of teaching and how they respond to another human. Second, a teacher, coach, mentor, leader or hero will possess character and momentum. They are essential in directing and helping you to accomplish your dreams.

Everyone at different stages in life will need that special person to intervene, motivate, coach and lead us into our destiny.

A leader will assist you in getting started. A leader will teach you how to concentrate on your own affairs, and teach you when to share your opinion.

The atmosphere and climate will automatically change and you must adjust.

Identifying a role model should be based on someone who has demonstrated positive thinking. **Parents should become representatives in their home.**

Leaders do not look for a task, instead the task will always find the leader.

A leader is capable of taking you to a higher plateau, the cause and affect are new beginnings.

A coach knows how to build your momentum, he teaches you the importance of becoming a team player and the essentials of discipline.

A coach never quits so we find ourselves not wanting to quit as we surpass our own expectations.

Its wise to consider both supernatural and physical power, it's your decision.

A leader does not have time to cover all subject matters, that's because they are busy teaching you to work hard, defeat fear, doubt and unbelief.

The Perfect Role Model

Great leaders are supported by and known for excellent forth coming leaders.

Your leader may be someone you have read, heard about or never seen, maybe they have accomplished something special.

Remember to test yourself "a reality check is not an option." If you are willing to listen, to think and rethink, to show respect, remember the rules of the game, commit yourself and think win-win, there's nothing that can stand in your way.

∞

IMPORTANT LIFE SKILLS

Winners

Winners will always give their clients what they want and need. It's not about what I like or what I have to offer. I can provide what you need.

A winner understands that records are established and will be challenged.

Don't quit

Now is the time to just do it

Winners dream and vision them self as a winner and never forget the positive affect of their thoughts

Winners dream and vision ways to bridge the gap between one another's unfinished dreams.

Rewards and an earned education

Create and restore relationships

∾

GO FOR THE GOLD!

Winners

If you want to be a winner the first thing you must do is change the way you think. I have never witnessed or heard a winner say, maybe I can do it. Winners and dreamers have a lot in common and sometimes it's hard to distinguish one from the other. A dreamer will hold fast to his vision and he establishes ground for it to occur. A winner has a clear vision of finishing and taking home the trophy and believes it will occur. They both possess strong traits that paddle them forward in life.

Winners seem to know what they want, and what's needed of them to break the record. It's a carryover of their lifestyle. They do not have to think about it because it's written in their hearts. There are many reasons for their behavior throughout their lives, but you know a winner when you see one. They will work at winning because the awards are given to the achievers. They are achievers in every background because they are equipped to handle the rules.

The stakes are high and there's weight resting on their shoulders, but they seem to concentrate on the bigger picture. Imagine that the dream is bigger than you, it has influence, power and a bright future when you consider it long term. Winners just keep on winning because it's in their DNA. They will set goals, become organized and chart out directions to see what's needed and the path they must journey. It's a work in progress and they are willing to meet those challenges and surpass records. They will say yes I can, I believe I can, I know I can, I have faith that I can, and now you know the rest of the story.

They know the importance of having a coach and that respect is a given. Respect yourself first and then you will learn to respect others. Accomplishments are rarely done alone and a winner understands well. They know the importance of listening and to have someone to assist with the ongoing pressure. Your coach is proud of you and your achievements, and the role that he and his staff played in making things happen. To be the best that I can be is needed.

Winners and dreamers see things the way they are and think of improvements. They embrace the idea that the impossible is possible, and their thoughts are, it might as well be me. If you want to become a winner at what you do start to hang with the winners and dreamers. You become part of your surroundings. A different results requires a paradigm shift. History has proven that nothing just happens or it's just co-incidental.

GO FOR THE GOLD!

IMPORTANT LIFE SKILLS

Entrepreneur–A Glimpse into Ownership & Wealth

Ownership-The state of being an owner. Legal title to something

Fellowship-Association, A body of persons having similar views or interests. Membership in a scholarly society.

Stewardship-A person entrusted with the management of the affairs of others

Membership-The members of an organization, collectively. The state of being a member

Leadership-The office or position of a leader. Ability to lead and leaders of a group.

Citizenship-Obligation, activities or attitudes, a group or persons with similar values for their country

Partnership-Joint interest or ownership. The state of being a partner. Contract of business associated with its partner

Entrepreneurship-One who undertakes to start or conducts an enterprise. Corporate board summing full control or risk over an enterprise, pensions, wages, restructuring, employment and environmental safety. Recognized for charitable giving

Discipleship-Signing on to all the above.

Hiring those considered to be potential gems, ready to be educated, innovators, enthusiastic, integrity and character means valued added.

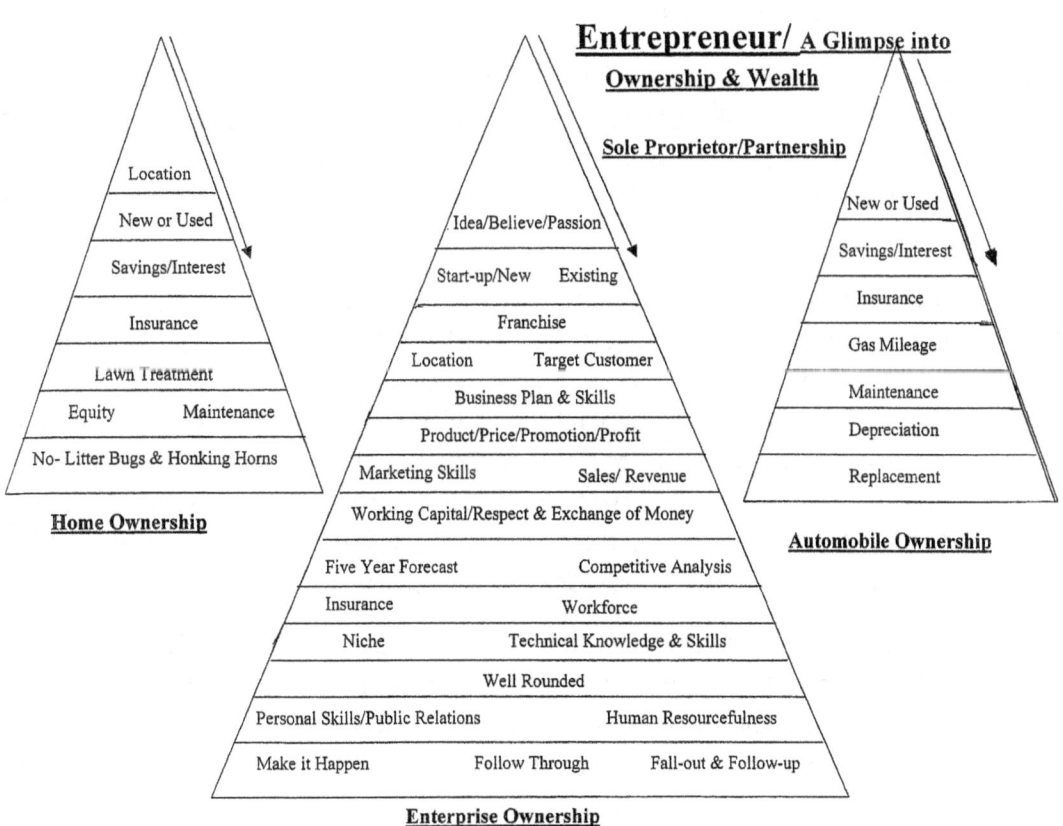

CEO SUMMIT

The Executive Branch & Entrepreneurs

Thank you for sharing your valuable time with me on a sensitive but urgent matter. The United States has embarked and currently going through an economic state of repair. History has often proven that we are a nation of hope, extended arms, faith and the best of the best. When the need arises or a call to action, we are known for our ability to unify for the common good of our nation and the world.

I am a new kid on the block as far as entrepreneurship, however this session today is fitting for all colleague. As you may have already heard or read about the unfavorable statements concerning the welfare of our country. Will we sit idle and do nothing, or will we recall our history and rise to the occasion?

I think it's only fitting for us to refresh our memory and address leadership, entrepreneurship, stewardship, partnership, fellowship, membership, ownership and citizenship. Its also a good time to address solidarity and volunteerism. Rewarding bad behavior does not necessarily speak for an entire corporation. A refresher course that includes the fellowship is sometimes needed when making tough decisions and sound judgement. It's you and your title who will share great responsibility for your organization's to get things done and done correctly.

The sum is always greater than its parts which bring me to solidarity. Why not share in the development of an Economic Recovery Plan for 2009. Your corporation automatically becomes a part of the whole as favorable statements reach the media. The donations would be used to assist our corporation with health care, education and employment. I'm reminded that some organizations retain an imaginary black book. Inside the book are profiles of the work force for excellence, the cream of the crops, creativity and talents, diverse qualified, college and leadership skills and much more. Also included are strategies for their investment growth in the organization.

As executive thought leaders and having received mastermind training, being accountable to your organization and to the fellowship should not be overlooked. In turn for carrying out our responsibilities we receive the gift of discipleship.

Own Your "Future Entrepreneurship"

Idea/ Belief/ Passion

If you can dream it you can see it and if you can see it continue to make it happen

Why not own your own business, home, automobile and assets?

Everyone at birth receives gifts and talents to get wealth and function

An education out of poverty may prove to be a wise investment

Organized and direction charts are useful and needed

Well rounded personality

An understanding of various relationship's are attributes that mirror character

Entrepreneur ownership and leadership are better

IMPORTANT LIFE SKILLS

Diversity

To view diversity as an exemption, not important or does not have an impact on one's life is an under statement

Imagine being position on the frontline of the battlefield all that's required is assistance.

We are blessed and honored to live on beautiful planet Earth, its up to you and I to preserve and educate others that diversity is alive, improving and turning back is not an option. We must try to show unconditional concerns, demonstrate and believe we can.

Diversity is best said when we connect at the right time, to the right degree, for the right reason and purpose and with the right people

Diversity challenges favoritism

Diversity

Diversity exist in many forms including food, music, people, places and nature.

During a crisis diversity may be defined as being position on the front line of a battlefield. All that matters is assistance.

Diversity clearly defines the Milky Way Galaxy and Solar Systems.

A diverse nation will naturally receive value added and bonuses.

Diversity is very much a part of America's way of life. As a leading nation of democracy, diversity must be transparent so that other nations will embrace their own possibilities.

Consider your mere presents in a diverse atmosphere and climate, it will set the tone.

Lewis and Clark's Expedition proved that diversity played a key role in their success, as team players, voting rights and human rights.

The big secret is inside you, you do things because it's the right thing to do.

Diversity challenges favoritism.

Diverse people are genuinely the light of the world because they embrace and understand, they study and they learn, they teach and they master without fear of cultural differences.

The only thing you have to fear is fear itself and not diversity. Diversity is alive and doing well, but needs some improvements in our homeland.

The Olympic games are excellent examples of diversity. One size does not fit all.

It's not a mistak e or accidental that we were created to be diverse. There are good and not so good people in the world, but they are not of one group.

Diversity is not present where harsh discrimination, intimidation, racism and hatred exist.

IMPORTANT LIFE SKILLS

Seniors are Precious Assets

Seniors share their wisdom with family, transition individuals, children and the world

Seniors share a common bond. They also share their faith in so many special ways.

Seniors have experienced life and know first hand the correct way to assist you to mastery

Seniors wear their thinking caps on their head for independence

Seniors have learn to ask if there is a stony heart within to please remove it and replace it with hope, joy, faith, love and kindness

We must show them love, respect and honor

We must never under estimate their values, morals and self worth

Seniors are Precious Assets

Seniors are like trees in many ways; their roots are deeply embedded
Both are experienced at weathering storms.

Seniors may have many off springs; trees have many seedlings.

Seniors nature their off spring with wisdom, teachings and love. Trees are calm, filled with a cycle of colorful beauty and full of life.

Seniors have many important and different purposes; grace also for their eternal life. Trees have important and different purposes; evidence also of an abundant life.

Don't be confused or fear the aging process, one hundred and twenty years of age can be realistic.

They supported unions, helped to establish important laws that we currently benefit from. Seniors served in the military, participated in mass communications and transportation, voting and civil rights, the space age, electronic technology, laser advancements and medical breakthrough. After completion of the information age and super highway now they are participating in the recommendation age. Thank you yesterday's seniors, who entered the workforce in the twentieth century, for your involvement in shaping more history than any other generation in America.

Seniors support their families in good times and bad times. They cook special meals, are great story tellers, provide home remedies for the sick, and they are not boastful. Seniors pray for you and they make you laugh in difficult times. Grandchildren love to share their family affairs with seniors because they know how to keep secrets.

Seniors do not ask or seek much attention, but they certainly deserve it. Call them daily and send or take flowers while they are still alive. Make room for them with family, united to care and see them through life's difficulties. Don't forget about them because after they are gone there will always be a void.

Seniors enjoy and look forward to birthday parties, a vacation, church events, grandchildren, family reunions, a trip to the park, a ride in the car, sports, movies, senior social society and the arts.

IMPORTANT LIFE SKILLS

African and American History/Who are you?

African American History and American History are the same. Both are unique in their struggles for and against freedom

Life is composed by the choices we make

Parents should give their young adult children a proper record for identification and history

Never again should a human-being be classified as a slave.

Forgiveness and faith are powerful

In spite of captivity slaves were taught English and Christianity

Learn to be proud of your heritage and lineage

∽

African and American History/Who are you?

Great emphasis should be placed on the importance of recognizing your family. It's the oldest distinguished group on earth. The most common family is a succession of persons connected by blood. Family connection reveals who you are. A family that recognizes and participates in family unity is more likely to stay united.

Free black people lived in America before the slave trade begin. In the sixteenth century, we find black explorers along the Mississippi Valley, and the areas known as New Mexico and South Carolina. The most celebrated black explorer was a gentlemen by the name of Esteban. In the 1530s he traveled and explored the Southwest. In 1619 twenty Africans landed in the colony of Virginia. They were not slaves, but became willing indentured servants, as were white settlers. They were bound to an employer for a limited number of years. The vast majority of blacks were taken captivity as cargo for the sole purpose of slavery. Consent and disgrace from African tribal leaders in exchange created a trade agreement with Spain and Portugal. The Middle Passage describes the casualties and suffering Africans slaves endured during their voyage.

Africans slaves are the only immigrants to travel to the America's not of their own free will. The most significant aspect of slavery was they were taught Christianity and granted freedom to worship. According to the United States Constitution slavery was prohibited. Both the North and South would experience heavy casualties.

The South was and remains to this day very powerful because they won the right, under the constitution, to count their slave population and received extra votes or three-fifths. Although the South received extra voting power, slaves were never represented. The primary reason for the Civil War is conclusive, the ownership of slaves as property.

Without the former signing of the United States Constitution there would not be as we know today a Union. The North was liberal and favored an interpretation granting the federal government expanded powers. The conservative South wanted to reserve undefined powers to individual states. Years of quarreling proved unsuccessful.

African and American History/Who are you?

The Confederate States, totaling eleven southern states, seceded from the Union. The northern and western states totaling twenty-three was supported by the federal government. The North fought against the South to preserve the Union. The South fought to win recognition as an independent nation and to retain slavery.

The North and West would experience an economical boom from the federal government to build roads, railroads and canals. Another issue was the opening of lands in the West. The new law would distribute such western lands in small lots, this would enhance development of the new section. The South opposed any such law because it aided the free farmers rather than the slave holding plantation owners. The North wanted a higher tariff to protect manufacturing. The South wanted a lower tariff that favored trade of its cotton for cheap foreign goods.

༄

IMPORTANT LIFE SKILLS

Death–The Loss of Someone Special

Write the deceased individual a note

Beware of depression

Candle light vigil

Grief and memories will strike at any time

Time will not always be spent in the same manner as before

Death
The Loss of Someone Special

What can be done to ease the mental pain of a loss? I tried to live an obedient lifestyle and look what happen. Will I ever see those I dearly loved again? Is that the end of our relationship? Who can I blame? Will there ever be closure? These are some of the questions we are faced with in dealing with death.

Without a death processing cycle the resurrection could never be justified. Death is an equal opportunity employer when confronted with the final stages of life. Whether it's a family member, a special friend, someone who inspired you, several lives loss or your special hero, we still experience grief.

Sorrow cannot be measured in length, depth or periods with another individual. Everyone grieves and mourns differently. We are in search of comfort and peace that surpasses our understanding. Some people refer to mourning and preparation for burial as a home going celebration. There's joy and sadness during this event because the deceased individual is no longer suffering and believed to be in a better place.

A planned memorial with love ones and friends seem to boost everyone's morale. It's thoughtful to assemble afterwards for a reception, for support and a brief chat. It shows that you still care and the deceased member will always be remembered. Respect is shown in many ways including placed flowers at the gravesite and a moment of silence is acknowledged. A thank you card for those in attendance will always make a statement of warmth and sincerity.

There are lessons to be learned when an infant is born into the family or death of a family member occurs. It raises our level of consciousness when a miracle equivalent to birth takes place. Before the final stage in association with death, confession time still remains. Why wait? However you choose to acknowledge both death and birth, it's worth consideration. We make plans for the new arrival, but it's equally as important to plan in advance for your burial. Documents for prearranged request should be made available when needed or let your final request be known publicly to the responding persons.

Death The Loss of Someone Special

Longevity has its place in life and we desire it for our self and love ones. One can only imagine that eternal life is greater.

We will cherish the fond memories of life before death of those we loved. We may need a support group occasionally to assist us back to reality. Acquaintances, friends and extended family relationships may help, but it does not improve much over night. Time seems to position you on a track to recovery. Time and prayer will help to heal the circumstances surrounding death, but there will always be a void. However, life must go on because there is plenty to do associated with living and interaction with others.

IMPORTANT LIFE SKILLS

Parenting

Become a role model for your child

Both parents must agree to walk together in harmony and peace

Communication works

Become the parent and not your child's best friend

Tell your children that they are special and how fortunate you are to share life with them

Both parents share in the responsibility for raising their child

Spend quality time with the family

Parenting

A human being will rely on his mind to govern himself. Parents desire the best for their children; and rely on their heart to govern their children. The heart speaks the spoken words.

A mother begins to bond with her child during early pregnancy. She recognizes the experience as a miracle from above. Both father and mother must agree to share in the responsibility of raising their child. Parents must teach their children to respect the female's womb that is responsible for infants birth.

Wise parents will create an atmosphere and climate in the home for their off spring to be blessed through four generations based on their belief. They will teach their children to obey the laws, establish positive relationships and important life skills. For accuracy sexuality empowerment needs to be discussed in the home.

Parents must observe their own lifestyle to determine what example they are modeling for their children. Spend quality time on how to overcome obstacles and improving character.

Parents are their children's first teachers. Be careful not to get involved in the transfer of power. As a parent you don't want to loose control and consequently render your power over to the child. All family members must learn how to express their love for one another. If this does not occurs the family member who's bank account fail to be replenish, but experience all withdrawals will suffer emotional.

Parents must consider the name that will represent their child. When he is of age explain to him the meaning, the significance and why you chose it. Both parents must agree through prayer and faith for their child's deliverance. It's very important that family members bond. Parents must establish peace, eliminate chaos and maintain order in their home. Confusion will not be tolerated. The family, extended family and church family are assets. Learn to bury disturbances and mishaps, they are not equivalent or representative to a family's sacrifice for bonding purposes.

Parenting

Parenting can be challenging because you play an important role in nurturing and developmental growth for your child. Never place limitations on your child's dream to succeed, it's a blessing to have a dreamer in the home. It's your job as a parent to assist the child with the least amount of disruptions.

As parents we recognize that each child has a compliant or strong will spirit. Your involvement during the formative years are crucial. All family members are individuals and they have their own unique personalities. The same approach for teaching may not apply or be regarded for all siblings. Don't allow fear and doubt to discourage you, but seek others help. Parent's rewards may include love and enjoyable relationships.

IMPORTANT LIFE SKILLS

Children and Adults Physically Challenged Contend with Survivor Skills

Life learned lessons are direct, reality, hope, faith and rejoice

No matter what the outcome will be "life or death," you can have victory

Never stop believing for your miracle. It's not uncommon to hear about or witness a miracle, they happen everyday

Enjoy each day and live today as if there is no tomorrow. Live the fullness of life.

We love you and want what's best for you

Death is part of life's processing cycle.

Children and Adults Physically Challenged Contend with Survivor Skills

Being diagnosed with a chronic illness is a shock. There are no easy solutions when confronted with an illness. Remember to take one step and one day at a time. Stay focused, hope and trust for a brighter day. It is not the end; you can get through it based on your belief, medical teams, hospital staff, and social centers, family, friends and a positive attitude. A crisis allows you to grow with meaning and purposes. The choice is yours if you desire victory.

Helpful Tips for Children with Chronic Illness
Know your physical capabilities and limitations.
Learn to accept your diagnoses of a chronic illness and know that it was not your fault.
Learn to control the illness and not the other way around.
Use others when needed to help with missed schooling.
Be honest with your friends and advise them when you are not feeling well.
Accept that you may be limited in extra curricular activities.
Know that you are special, one spirit, one soul and God does not create junk.
Maintaining some form of exercise daily is important.
Acknowledge purposes for your life; get the help you need to fulfill your destiny.
Obtain a driver's license and become a responsible driver for convenient transportation.
Maintain a proper diet.

Helpful Tips for Adults with Chronic Illness
Educate your spouse or significant other on survivor and assistance skills.
As you grow wiser consider if there are risks associated with pregnancy.
Transfer more responsibility from your parents or caregiver to yourself.
Know which jobs are suitable and available based on your physical condition.
Consider investing in a recliner chair and access to control cooling and heating.
The family must be informed of your needs and concerns for emotional help.

Children and Adults Physically Challenged Contend with Survivor Skills

Become independent, it improves your confidence.
Develop a strong and intimate relationship with your choice of powers.
Its normal to cry.
Inform your employer of your condition after medical benefits enrollment occurs.
Allow others to pray for you, accept a prepared meal, flowers or cards, and allow others to visit if only for a brief moment.
Fear not

∽

IMPORTANT LIFE SKILLS

Anger Management–A Wise Man Controls his Anger

A successful life will not occur if the odds are against you due to anger

Anger is a cancer causing emotion that destroys you and your surrounding if left untreated

Anger does not define whose right and whose wrong. It can lead to jail time, separation, division, hatred and murder

The one who speaks the loudest is the one that is heard. Most of the time they don't know that they don't know

Speak softly but always beware

Forgiveness is powerful even when we do not understand

Replace anger with positive behavior, and refuse to allow anger to settle in your heart. It will lead to a stony heart.

Most of the time we are sorry that we allowed anger to under mind our will. We don't desire or wish you mishap, but just stay away.

Change is not always easy and the sooner we realize it things will become more manageable. Those who are willing to incorporate change are more likely to succeed.

Anger Management–A Wise Man Controls his Anger

How do you isolate the problem from the truth? Who will admit the real truth? Often the real problem is never discussed and a change in subjects will occur. That's because a lie, an undesirable habit, and deceit may boost another's chance of becoming the winner. Don't get caught up in the game.

Be mindful that everyone does not apologize in the same manner. For some it is communicated orally, for others it is communicated through one's actions. If its from your heart, the accused remorse is shown. The recipient is responsible for accepting the apology and moving on. Ask yourself, "Are those individuals intentions meant to hurt me?"

One of the greatest rewards is turning anger into forgiveness. Time, patience and a willing conscious, having nothing to do with right or wrong, will help to heal the damages that occurred. Sometimes you must keep silent, recognizing the situation is blocked and no detour is in sight. Anger is an emotion that consumes the body and mind if not dealt with properly. We are born with a natural instinct to do evil, but we must be trained to overcome evil with good.

Non violence can move a nation forward into a positive direction. Poverty, a disease unattended, can cripple a nation; violence unattended can destroy a movement. State the facts and the issues and remain focused. No one wins minus long and short term positive motives. Always remember to show respect.

Learn to anonymous report the truth to the proper authority. This will help to reduce the crime rate of a repeated offender whose actions are to deliberately victimize another.

When you approach conflict in the workplace there are appropriate ways to address your concerns. If you choose the inappropriate way you could be joining the anger party. There are ways to conduct a healthy discussion that will achieve positive results. If you choose the correct way, remember to always follow the chain of command. As the issue escalates allow yourself an opportunity to review from all sides.

Anger Management—A Wise Man Controls his Anger

The next time you feel anger coming on and you are ready to respond ask yourself; "If this is the right time, the right reason and purpose, with the right person and to the right degree"?

Never feed on anger. Anger feeds off of trouble and problems that eventually leads to rage. Always attempt to defuse anger. Rage may prolong or postpone the solution. Anger knows no racial class nor educational boundaries. Inconveniences or missed opportunities may be associated with poor judgement. People who will seek a counselor's advice and follow recommendations are more likely to overcome anger.

IMPORTANT LIFE SKILLS

A Sound Mind

A clear and honest conscious may unlock the door to a sound mind

A sound mind consists of peace, wisdom and love

Love is charity. When love shows up it takes center stage and everything else is position backstage.

You are not crazy if you believe in miracles

The release of others being held by others under self-control must cease.

Divine success and divine expectancy are definitely needed for a sound mind

A drive-thru, breakthrough to submit your concerns does not exist in today's world. Assisting the poor and others with kindness, gentleness, humble and compassion increases probability for a sound mind

A Sound Mind

Life should include organization and directions, these are essentials for the journey we face. An epiphany clears the way when we are reminded that our life is composed of choices. A sound mind plays a significant role in how well we function. A sound mind consists of peace, wisdom, patience and mastery. Consider a clear mind and conscious that speaks to you positively and walks you through targeted circumstances.

Turning back for the majority is not an option. Always believe in yourself and don't quit. A sound mind is an asset and a terrible thing to waste. Ordinary people do extraordinary things everyday so don't allow anyone to use the fear factor and dominate your thinking. You are all that you were created to be and you have a bright future.

Learning how to work with others does not mean your character has made you a star, but your character has valuable traits that contribute to your ability to work through many circumstances. We cannot prepare in advance for negative forces wanting to invade our lives. Experience and awareness for critical moments are essential in decision making. Learning how to prioritize issues of importance, urgency and factoring in a timetable means proficiency and stability. Understanding when your plate is full, what areas your expertise covers and when to say, "No" demonstrates critical thinking.

The mere idea that love never fails and is replenished forever is incredible. Who we really are is revealed in our character. Why do we participate in acts of kindness with some of the same people we experienced hurt? Love over shadows hatred. We move at an accelerated pace when we choose to walk in forgiveness oppose to vengeance. Evil is harsh and absorbs the inner man's soul. Expect nothing for selfish motives.

The mind is the battlefield. Clinical depression is more than just feeling bad. It should not be mistaken for, although similar, mental illness because they are not the same. Depression is a disease that no one wants to talk about. Depression is a medical disorder, a combination of physical and psychological symptoms. About ten percent of U. S. citizens will experience some form of clinical depression while living a normal life.

Depressive illness exist in our communities, in the workplace and may include family members. Always leave yourself a way out, walk in love, power and a sound mind.

IMPORTANT LIFE SKILLS

Wellness–Emotional and Physical

A balanced lifestyle is important

Create and restore relationships now, tomorrow is not promised

Become a good listener and a critical thinker. Constructive criticism is effective when used purposeful and privately as a tool.

Beware and stay away from negative action, negative emotions and negative personal growth

Move with success from being dependent to independence. Learn not to agree with everything someone may say. It indicates that someone is not an independent thinker and does not have their own opinion.

Do you have friends? If rightly so make time for friendship and fellowship.

The ultimate goal is to enhance your abilities to successfully incorporate positive behavior, positive emotions and physical wellness by way of interdependence.

Maneuverability is critical when trying to go from location A to location B. First you must believe that location B exist and it is achievable.

Wellness–Emotional and Physical

Sending someone an e-mail is a great way to stay in touch. A social life is important and should be factored into a wholesome lifestyle. A conference on a cruise with a group will allow you to stay connected while having fun. Corporate, Toastmaster and investment conferences are excellent ways to stay empowered, informed and meet with your group. If you lack maturity on important matters or have low-self esteem, and would like to see personal growth in other areas of your life, consider plans for group like settings.

Have you decided what is important to you and attainable? This is the beginning of your journey down the yellow brick road. Don't worry about how to get there, but why it's important that you go there. The how will show up later as you quest forward.

Negative emotions are a nuisance, beware of them. Positive emotions can uplift and help you to heal. Positive emotions will also build your confidence and hope for the future. Recognize that it's normal to experience sadness, it means you are hurt, broken or tenderhearted. First, when you receive bad news, try to get all the facts, repeating information is not easy. Second, you must maintain a sincere conversation not allowing things to escalate into wide spread gossip. We may loose valuable information every time we attempt to pass it on to another individual.

We may mistakenly rely on another individual to make us happy. Because life is not predictable and not always fair, happiness may be associated with how well you handle stress. Learning how to stay focus may impose a certain amount of stress. Trying to make another individual happy means you possess valuable assets. Happiness is highly regarded and comes from the mind and soul. There are many elements to include in our happiness, but a normal lifestyle is determined based solely on your decisions. If you will agree with everything I propose, it's an indication that someone has rendered their responsibility to think and decision making over to someone else.

Develop a habit of being kind to oneself. You must learn how to meet some of your own needs. You are not being selfish if you treat yourself a few hours each month. Work on a sensible budget that allows you to do

Wellness–Emotional and Physical

something meaningful with family or friends frequently. Allow for a long distance call as an example to a former co-worker.

As you incorporate wellness into your lifestyle an epiphany is transparent and material things will become less important. The best things in life are achievable through practice, mastery and relationships. The best things in life are priceless, a price tag placed on an item cannot be defined as priceless. Don't wait until an individual is no longer present and wish that; if only I had taken more time things could have turned out differently.

IMPORTANT LIFE SKILLS

A Moment in Time

Recognize and seize the moment when opportunities arise

The International Date Line does not represent the day the world stood still

There would not be any job opportunities, developmental growth, exploring, learning from your mistakes and no reason to think

Communication works

Learn to read the lines, read in between the lines and read beyond the lines.

Your mission is to live life to its fullness today

A Moment in Time

As long as the sun will provide the earth with day light, and the moon will provide the earth light at night, and as long as the mighty forces of gravity continues to secure humanity on the earth surface, changes will occur. There is what is known as the International Dateline. The International Dateline separates today from tomorrow, the past from the future, realities from dreams, hope from despair and faith from doubt.

The International Dateline is present with us now, **for it is just as imaginary at this moment in time, as it is in its proper setting.** Yet, what is real concerning this line is if you stood directly on it you would freeze time. What lies ahead could never be explored, and the opportunities that wait could never be grasp, if we fail to seek out our visions, hopes and dreams. We are constantly striving for a new day, and we must also remember that our future is composed from new ideas and new realities.

Let's suppose your employer's mission statement reads: "We are dedicated to being the world's best in class at bring people together, giving them easy access to each other and to the information and services they want and need, anytime and anywhere." Now vision yourself as being the world best at what you do. One important question to keep in mind is am I trying to make money or solve problems or both? There's much potential, opportunities and consideration to examine. **A moment in time may be your golden opportunity with no strings attached.** The whole is always greater than its parts alone.

Dreamers will hold fast in their heart to their visions and siege the moment to accomplish realities. **Without vision you may fail to see opportunities all in a moment in time.** Without hope, or without a dream, or without a goal, and without a belief system, "Wisdom for Intrinsic Fulfillment" cannot assist you. We gain momentum when we believe that location B exist and with determination to find a way or detour to arrive there.

In addition, as we accomplish our mission you will experience joy and happiness, all in a moment in time. Its a win-win situation, no turning back because it's not an option. I'll see you at the top!

<u>If I can teach important life skills and</u>

<u>if you can learn important life skills</u>

<u>If you will apply and act on important life skills</u>

<u>Your investment as it applies to Wisdom</u>

<u>for Intrinsic Fulfillment has a genuine</u>

<u>connection to your future</u>

<u>Happiness is peace that passes all understanding</u>

To Say Thanks

    Willa R. Boykin

SURVEY QUESTIONNAIRE

Wisdom for Intrinsic Fulfillment

What is your single most important question _____

What is your single most biggest fear_____

What are you expecting from this training_____

If you are trying to arrive at location B do you believe it exist_____

Are you ready and prepared to go to your next level_____

༄

www.ingramcontent.com/pod-product-compliance
Lightning Source LLC
LaVergne TN
LVHW061216060426
835507LV00016B/1971

9 780976 532903